Touch

Written by Mandy Suhr

Illustrated by Mike Gordon

The Senses

Hearing
Sight
Smell
Taste
Touch

First published in Great Britain in 1993
by Wayland (Publishers) Ltd

This edition printed in 2001 by Hodder Wayland,
an imprint of Hodder Children's Books
Revised in 2007 by Wayland, an imprint of Hachette Children's Books

Hachette Children's Books
338 Euston Road, London NW1 3BH

Series Editor: Mandy Suhr
Book Editor: Francesca Motisi
Editorial Assistant: Zoe Hargreaves
Consultants: Jane Battell and Richard Killick
Cover Designer: Elaine Wilkinson

British Library Cataloguing in Publication Data
Suhr , Mandy
 Touch - (Senses series)
 I. Title II. Gordon, Mike III. Series
 612.8

Paperback ISBN 978-0-7502-5276-8

Printed and bound in China

Contents

Close your eyes.
Touch some things
around you.

4

How many different
kinds of things can
you feel?

Some things feel hard...

some things feel soft.

Some things
feel smooth...

8

some things feel rough.

Some things feel dry...

or wet...

10

or even slimy!

The way something
feels is called its
texture. Some things have
a different texture on
the outside from that
on the inside.

You can feel things when you touch them because we have special touch detectors in our skin. These are very small and are hidden in your skin.

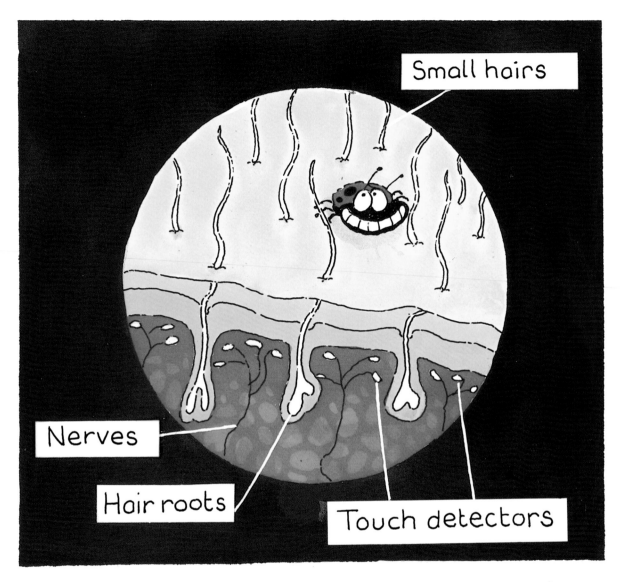

To see the touch detectors you need
a very strong microscope.

When you touch something,
the nerves carry messages
to your brain.

Then your brain uses these messages to work out what you are touching.

Nerves also send messages
to your brain if you touch
something that feels
hot or cold.

Your brain uses these messages and tells you to move if something is too hot!

Some parts of our bodies, like our fingers and lips, are better at feeling than other parts. This is because there are more detectors here.

Can you find
out which other
parts are good
at feeling?

Sometimes people who cannot see use touch to help them. They can feel what a person looks like even though they can't see them!
This is because your brain can also work out what something looks like from the messages it is sent by your nerves.

My friend Lizzy can read by touching!
She can't see the special letters.

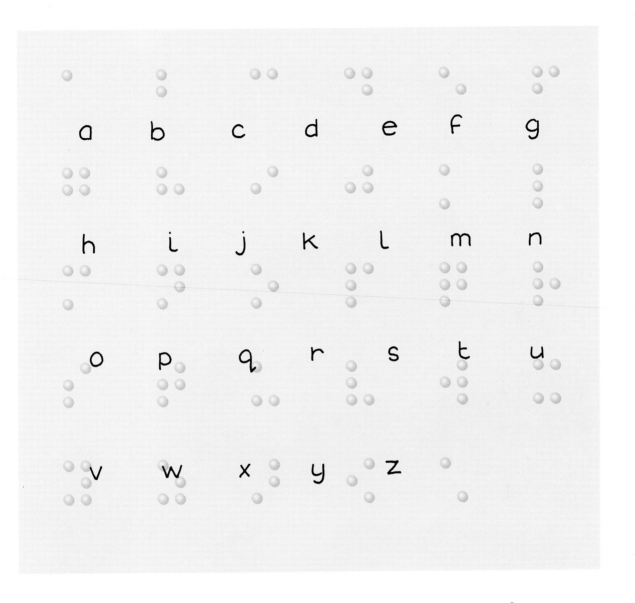

But she can feel them because they are raised on the page.

What is your favourite texture?
Can you describe how it feels?

Play this game with a friend.
Make a 'feely box'.

Can your friend guess what is
in it just by feeling?

Notes for adults

'The Senses' is a series of first information books specially designed for the early stages of reading. Each book has a simple, factual text and amusing illustrations, combining reading for pleasure with fact-finding.

The content of the book addresses the requirements of the National Curriculum for Science, Key Stage One. The series takes a closer look at the human body, explaining very simply how we use each of our senses to learn about the world around us. This book explores the sense of touch.

The books are equally suitable for use at home or at school. Here are some suggestions for extension activities to complement the learning in this book.

1. Design a feeling/touch game using the one in this book as an example. This activity promotes collaborative learning when carried out in small groups. It encourages hypothesizing and discussion, both important language skills. Children can also be

encouraged to design a scoring system to incorporate practise of numerical skills.

2. Practise grouping and ordering skills. Textures can be grouped in sets and ordered within their group. This involves designing experiments, discussion, using mathematical sets and provides a variety of opportunities for recording of results eg graphs, tables, setting up and using data bases.

3. Design experiments to test which parts of your body are most receptive to touch. Use a feather to gently touch various body parts. Record which are most sensitive.

4. Make tactile collages using materials with different sorts of textures.

5. Design posters that warn other children about things they should not touch.

6. Record different textures using 'rubbing' techniques. Which rubbings are most successful? Why?

Books to read

Touch! Edited by Lois Rock (Lion Publishing, 1991)

Touch and Feel by Doug Kincaid and Peter Coles

(Rourke Pub Group, 1983)

What Happens When You Touch and Feel

by Joy Richardson (Evan Brothers, 1992)

My First Look at Touch by Toni Rann

(Random House Children's Books, 1990)

Your Senses by Angela Royston (F. Lincoln, 1993)

Senses (Criss-Cross) by Hazel Songhurst

(Wayland, 1993)

All About Your Senses by Donna Bailey

(Heinemann, 1990)